CONVERSATIONAL
CAMOUFLAGE

Oratory Discretion and Pretexting for Behavioral Concealment

Matthew Dermody

Conversational Camouflage:
Oratory Discretion and Pretexting for Behavioral Concealment

Copyright © 2018 by Matthew Dermody

ISBN-13: 978-1984966872
ISBN-10: 1984966871

Printed in the United States of America

Cover art design by Matthew Dermody

Front cover face photo courtesy of Kristina Flour via Unsplash.com.
Camouflage pattern courtesy of www.pixabay.com.
Back cover photo by Matthew Dermody

All rights reserved. This book or any parts thereof may not be reproduced in any form, stored in a retrieval system, or transmitted in any form by any means-- electronic, mechanical, photocopy, recording, or otherwise--without prior written permission of the author and publisher, except as provided by United States of America copyright law.

Neither the author nor publisher assumes any responsibility or liability for the use or misuse of the information contained within this book; intentional or otherwise. The contents are for informational purposes only.

Other Published Works by Matthew Dermody

Books:
Hidden Success: A Comprehensive Guide to Ghillie Suit Construction
Appear to Vanish: Stealth Concepts for Effective Camouflage and Concealment
Gray Man: Camouflage for Crowds, Cities, and Civil Crisis
Hidden In Plain Sight: A Prepper's Guide to Hiding, Discovering, and Scavenging Diversion Safes and Caches
Gray Woman: A Woman's Guide to Gray Man Tactics

Website Resources: (www.hiddensuccesstactical.com)
Civilian and Military Camouflage Patterns – General Editor
Inexpensive Winter Ghillie Blanket
3 Reasons to Stock up on Halloween Make-Up
The Tactical Drawbacks of High-Definition (HD) Camouflage Patterns

Guest Blogs:
Six Materials for Field Expedient Natural Camouflage – www.willowhavenoutdoor.com
Do You Really Need a Ghillie Suit? – www.itstactical.com
Build Your Own Ghillie Suit for Under $75 – www.itstactical.com
Practical Alternatives for Buried Survival Caches – www.survivalschool.us

Magazines:
Backwoodsman Magazine, <u>*Vanishing Act*</u>, Nov/Dec 2018, Vol. 39, Issue No. 6

ACKNOWLEDGEMENTS

I would like to thank my friends and colleagues who contributed some of their personal stories and experiences to further explain and put into context the concepts presented within this book.

Many thanks are due to my friends, Shawn Swanson and John Wisch. Their counsel and discussions have aided me immensely in the writing of this book. Their willingness to make themselves available when I had questions is truly appreciated.

No acknowledgement section would be complete without the inclusion of my wonderful wife and our twin girls. Their faithful support and encouragement are essential to my writing success. I love you very much.

REVIEWS

"Dermody has expanded his research into the realm of deception, concealment, and persuasion during verbal engagements. This work will be an interesting addition and perspective to the subject."

— **Troy Lettieri**, US Army and SOF veteran

"...hammered home the most important factors of OPSEC and PERSEC...behavioral traits that usually give people away quickly...this book picks up where (Dermody's) other books left off.."

— **David Everhart**, Certified Master Scout Tracker GT6M and GTSB Lead Examiner, Eastern United States

"Matthew Dermody is the undisputed master of the subtle art of camouflage. From practical application to the evasive exchange of intelligence, Dermody's books offer a master class for those...looking to hide in plain sight."

— **Josh Haney**, No Fate Survival

DISCLAIMER:

Neither the author nor the publisher assumes any responsibility or liability for the use or misuse of the information contained and presented within this book, intentional or otherwise. Readers are advised to follow all applicable federal, state, and local laws. The contents are for informational purposes only.

TABLE OF CONTENTS

Chapter 1 – THE PURPOSE OF BEHAVIORAL CAMOUFLAGE 1

Section I - Introduction

Chapter 2 – ▮▮▮ SITUATIONS ▮▮▮ ...11

Chapter 3 – SURENESS/SUSPICION ▮▮▮ 18

Chapter 4 – ▮▮▮ SECURITY ▮ 26

Section II - Green Zone

Chapter 5 – SIGNALING ▮▮▮ 33

Chapter 6 – ▮▮▮ SOCIAL SITES ▮▮▮ 38

Chapter 7 – ▮▮▮ STRATEGIC SHARING 44

Section III - Yellow Zone

Chapter 8 – ▮ SUPPRESSION ▮▮▮ 51

Chapter 9 – ▮▮▮ SELECTIVITY ▮ 56

Chapter 10 – ▮▮▮ SCRUTINY ▮▮▮ ...63

Chapter 11 – ▮ SIGNIFICANCE ▮▮▮ 67

Section IV - Red Zone

Chapter 12 – ████████████████ SILENCE 74

Chapter 13 – ██████████ SECRETS ████████████████ ...80

Chapter 14 – ████████████ SUBTERFUGE ████████. 85

Chapter 15 – ██████████████ SUBCONSCIOUS 91

Additional Resources 98

About the Author.. 100

"Death and life are in the power of the tongue..."

- Proverbs 18:21, *King James Bible*

CHAPTER ONE

THE PURPOSE OF BEHAVIORAL CAMOUFLAGE

Sometimes I wish I could just shut up. In all other instances, I would like to think more before I speak. Despite this confession, I imagine I am not alone in this regard. Most of my frustration regarding my desire to keep people out of my business stems from my inability to keep my mouth shut. In the opposite direction, revealing too much about me or giving greater explanation than what is needed is often the diagnosis. In an odd twist of self-inflicted irony, the nature of what I do and teach demands a certain degree of oratory clarification when someone asks what I do. I often wonder if others struggle with that same balance. How much information is **too much** information?

The real, private me *wants* to say, "None of your business!" while the pragmatic, entrepreneurial side of me *needs* to say, "Let me tell you about my business." Even trying to apply what I learned about operations security (OPSEC) during my six-year stint in the US Navy does not always produce consistent results. Good OPSEC skills require discernment, discipline, and vigilance. As such, this is a reinforcement of the notion that just as weapons systems and fieldcraft skills are perishable, solid

OPSEC is a perishable skill as well. Therefore, these skills should be practiced routinely.

My books have discussed and acknowledged a gradual progression from easy to difficult regarding the mastery of the subtleties surrounding camouflage and concealment. Behavior is one of the most difficult things to modify. Especially when dealing with behaviors that have become habit. We are creatures of habit and in order to "work smarter not harder," we often venture down the path of least resistance. The path is clear and well-travelled, but the ruts are made by followers, not leaders. It is necessary to step out of the ruts created and carved out by others. I am first to admit my need to do so, especially now that I have a growing readership and have people looking to me as a recognized expert in the subject of camouflage and concealment. I must push myself harder to pursue even more experience to compliment my research on the subject.

Despite my recognition by some as a subject matter expert (SME), I find it difficult to refer to myself as such. However, I have had many friends, colleagues, and esteemed mentors insist that I embrace the accolade and take ownership of the calling based on the research and work I have put towards the subject. This has inspired me to delve into the next aspect of camouflage and concealment that is the most difficult realm to master: behavior camouflage. So, how do we start a project like this? We need to break it down into bite-size concepts that can be individually analyzed, mentally chewed, and digested.

How do we conceal our behavior? Why is it important? When is it necessary? What circumstances preordain its implementation? This is a big task to undertake and a bigger challenge because it relates to behavior and behavior modification, to a certain degree. It is also a challenge for me on a personal level, as I find little difficulty in being physically able to blend into an environment with camouflage clothing or a ghillie suit. I can move about a city with relative anonymity just by obeying the laws and societal norms in the places I visit. However, changing behavior is difficult. If it were not, there would be no need for the countless self-help books and professionals in existence to help people overcome habits and undesired behavior.

The S's of Behavioral Camouflage. Illustration by author.

In the similar fashion in which I described the stealth concepts in both *Appear to Vanish* and *Gray Man*, this book will be no different. Each concept begins with the letter "S". The alliteration serves as a common denominator of sorts to all the other concepts explored in my previous books. The intent is to show the inter-dependence and correlation to the other concepts and how disguising communication and behavior are intrinsically linked to physical camouflage and concealment techniques.

The sampled redaction of the table of contents is a written and physical parallel we must perform mentally and verbally in real time. Redaction, for the uninitiated, is the purposeful deletion or removal of readable text or information within a document. It is generally done to prevent unwanted disclosure of highly sensitive, classified material. For most people, their only knowledge or contact with redacted information is through spy novels and movies. This real time implementation of this concept is what gives us the extreme level of difficulty to practicing good OPSEC.

We think and speak much faster than we can sometimes analyze or "proofread" what we say. Herein lays the trouble when we are unable to take back words we ought not to have spoken or regret saying, for whatever reason.

Conversational Camouflage intends to be more involved and in-depth than a simplistic, sarcastic summary telling readers to *"Shut up."* At the same time, it is not intended to be a drawn out or strained, creative outlet to discover how many unique ways to express that same sentiment. Nor is it intended to be a grand opus, encompassing and including all that pertains to psychological warfare, the use of propaganda, unconventional tactics, body language, psychology, or the various forms of deception. It is a simple introduction to the topic, giving the reader the opportunity to explore its various uses, while introducing the concepts behind conversational camouflage with a useful alliteration for easy remembrance.

While keeping one's mouth shut is a huge factor in behavior concealment, knowing what to say when silence is not an option, is equally important. This is where the concept of pretexting becomes an integral part of behavioral concealment. It is also applicable in enhanced interrogation scenarios, discussed later in Chapter 13.

It is important to understand and realize this book and the discussion of its contents is in direct conflict and opposition to the tenets of honesty, integrity, and truthfulness. It violates the doctrinal principles of many religious teachings, with a few exceptions. It has a certain level of open disregard to societal norms and civilized cultures. Deeply religious people may be taken aback by the methodology and implementation of these types of tactics. I am not advocating or condoning these things, merely pointing out their existence.

While I am far from the fabled integrity of George Washington's "I cannot tell a lie," I certainly believe one cannot not habitually and intentionally engage in these behaviors and expect to maintain *healthy* relationships with others. Relationships of any kind must be fostered and nurtured in trust. Any relationship, personal or professional, will be weakened or be destroyed by dishonesty. Once honesty and integrity are called into question, it is often difficult to restore. How many people do you know of personally whom someone has allowed back into their life at the same level of trust prior to the betrayal? You could probably count them on one hand, even if missing a finger or two. It simply does not happen and if/when it does, that behavior then becomes suspicious in and of itself.

However, this is not to say that certain levels of dishonesty or information withholding are intrinsically bad or does not exist. A dissatisfied employee, who yearns to open his or her own business, may not inform their employer of their desire to do so. This may be to avoid reprisals or premature dismissal. It may also be done to protect ideas from unscrupulous bosses who exploit the talents and hard work of their employees in an effort to advance the company.

I also believe there are consequences to be suffered when used inappropriately, while understanding the principles of self-preservation that often preclude some of these tactics. I often reference white lies with a little humor to explain this. Many of us have heard these types of examples. For instance, when a woman asks her husband, "Do these pants make me look fat?" or "Does this look okay?" The husband may respond with a different truth or fact that she did not specifically ask for. He may use a phrase to distract or create a conversational rabbit trail.

There are countless books written on communication shortcomings, not just between the two sexes, but combating communication breakdowns in general. While the purpose of those books is to have both parties understand each other and seeking to be understood, *Conversational Camouflage* openly admits to promoting the intentional confusion of one party to protect the safety and security of either information or people.

With all of that said, this question also demands an answer. Whom potentially benefits from the information contained within this book? The most obvious are foreign operatives and those working in the various intelligence agencies. There is a law enforcement component as well with officers engaged in undercover work. It also serves as a reinforcing guide for our deployed service-members in the military.

How does this apply to the everyday civilian? How does he or she benefit from this knowledge? It is no secret there are people involved in criminal activity. They look to use and exploit the personal information belonging to others. It makes sense that the information presented will better prepare people to avoid the attempts of criminals committing fraud and swindles. Protecting personal information such as one's social security number, bank accounts, passwords, and secure log-ins are just a few examples. What about those who have prepared for short and long-term disasters, do they have information to safeguard? The answer is, yes.

Surely, no one who has taken the time and effort to stockpile supplies wants to compromise those commodities by telling all of their neighbors about it. This is where the major benefit of OPSEC comes into focus. Admittedly, this is a target audience I want to reach with this book. It is of little value to go to tremendous effort to gather supplies, fortify your home, and prepare for uncertain times if one decides to run one's mouth carelessly concerning the types and amounts of those stockpiles. OPSEC is a vital necessity to these types of endeavors. However, there is a substantial amount of disregard for it on social media. I feel it needs to be addressed for the sake of those who don't possess the foundations of OPSEC currently.

Often, the best analogy for two and three level decision-making is the common traffic control device. Almost everyone, whether they are a driver or passenger, understands the three-colored light system used to control the flow of traffic. Green means go, yellow means slow down; prepare to stop, and red means stop. It is simple and effective.

The use of color codes to differentiate the various levels of threats is common in many facets of life, but the one I am reminded of and frequently use is the color code developed by the late Colonel Jeff Cooper regarding the combat mindset and its relationship to situational awareness.

THE COLOR CODE OF ORATORY DISCRETION

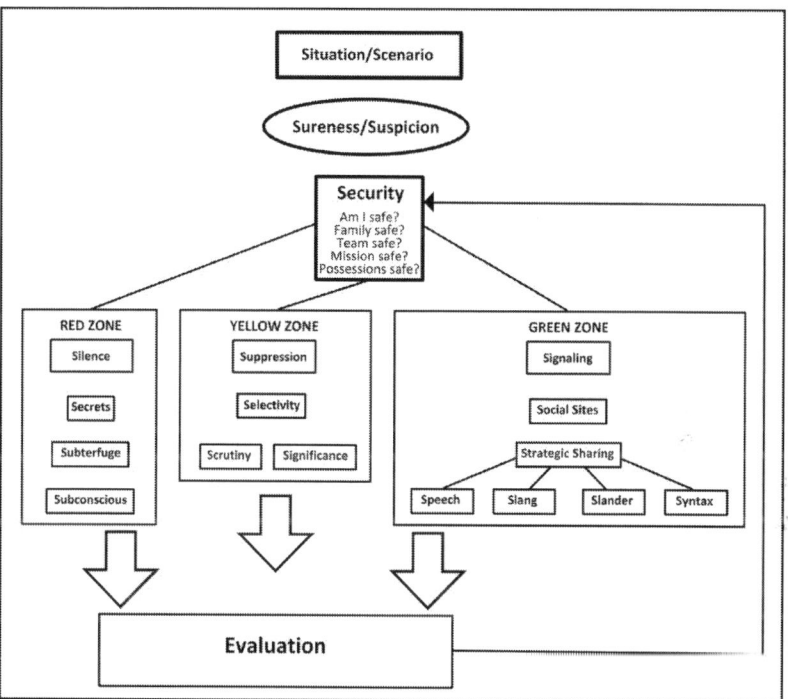

Information dissemination flow chart. Illustration by author.

Green Zone - In this zone, the dissemination of information is generally regarded as safe. However, safe is a somewhat subjective term, as some individuals are not as comfortable sharing certain types of information as others may be. Deciding to what extent you are willing and prepared to divulge such information is determined on an individual, case-by-case basis.

Yellow Zone - The Yellow Zone is the fulcrum, or balancing point tipping the decision scale in one direction or the other. Using this zone as a starting point gives people the opportunity to set their own course as to whether or not they want to earn trust. If they start in the Red Zone, the yellow becomes a potential bridge to the Green Zone.

Red Zone - This is the "no-go" zone. No critical or private information should be disseminated. People or situations relegated to this zone are not privileged or authorized to access the information you possess or intend to protect. Compromise in this zone can have serious consequences to mission or personal safety.

Despite its appearance as untrusting and maybe even hostile, until someone has earned your trust, it is probably better to start in the red zone. This gives you the best chance to protect vital information, while leaving room for the opportunity to vet potential collaborators or colleagues as necessary.

SECTION I

Introduction

CHAPTER TWO

SITUATIONS

Sometimes I am required (or politely obligated) to attend functions where my wife works. It is no secret that many of today's corporations and work environments have differing viewpoints on politics, religion, and all sorts of topics. This obviously affects what I say about what I do and my opinions on a whole slew of subjects considered socially taboo or which may be in direct conflict with workplace policies or agendas.

I personally despise these functions, as our arrival to such events is often prefaced with a sincere admonition to avoid discussing anything too controversial. My dislike for these types of functions stems from the requirement (based upon spousal request) of suppressing the "real" me. While it may not be pleasant for me, it does keep my wife gainfully employed without my opinions provoking unfavorable judgments towards her. Therefore, I must relinquish myself to the prospect of painting a non-threatening, conformist self-portrait that appears, on face value, to align with their ideals. Doing so avoids upsetting the status quo and the egos of self-proclaimed, intellectually superior people who hold copious amount of stock in their own professional propaganda.

However, I do try to see the unseen benefit in these events and use them as a chance to practice the tradecraft with little regard to how people view my including them unknowingly in these pretexting exercises. Most people would most likely object to being used in such a manner, even if no harm is intended or incurred. As an added bonus, I sometimes get to gather intelligence regarding the philosophies and belief systems that form the basis of their opinions, regardless of whether or not I share those same thoughts. People, in general, like to talk. They like talking about themselves, their accomplishments, qualifications, aspirations, and ideologies even more. People desire a sense of belonging because of how me are designed to interact socially. The more a person can validate their inclusion to whatever social circle they wish to join, the better their chances of being accepted into a particular group.

Communication skills and understanding body language are crucial to developing good OPSEC practices. Photo courtesy of www.pixabay.com

As with many things, the situations or scenarios you face are subjective based upon training, knowledge, and experience. However, there exists a fundamental truth in any dangerous situation. A threat is still a threat regardless of whether or not the person (intended victim) is trained, has knowledge, or experience in dealing with such threats.

There is no possible way to write every possible situation or scenario that warrants an OPSEC or PERSEC protocol. However, here is a short list to serve as examples.

- Granting membership into a survival group
- Restricting access to certain features, information, or supplies
- Denying Wi-Fi passwords
- Limiting computer and/or Internet access
- Isolation from key members or protected assets
- Withholding specific security procedures and protocols
- Blindfolding individuals to maintain the secrecy of locations
- Withholding information from the media and press because of pending/ongoing investigation
- The use of code words or ciphers

These are examples of the technique often referred to as compartmentalization. Compartmentalization is a fancy, multi-syllable word that simply means to avoid putting all of your eggs in one basket. This technique allows for the partitioning of information, preventing or minimizing whole disclosure of that information.

Each "compartment" contains its own unique parameters regarding the possession of proper security clearance (or level of trust) combined with a reasonably valid and necessary need to know. Need to know is just that; having a justifiable need to have access to the information for the carrying out or executing duties or objectives based on that information.

This sculpture is a stark reminder that someone is always listening. Even small pieces of conversations have the ability to paint broad, clear pictures. Photo courtesy of www.pixabay.com

As situations unfold, the primary beginnings of behavioral camouflage are put into motion. They begin with a rapid gathering of facts, personal experiences, and yes, even stereotypes and biases. This information comes together and forms what is known commonly as the first impression.

All situations and scenarios need to have an objectively conceived risk management component put into place. Knowing the risks and potential outcomes help minimize harm and maximize safety and security. The following is an excellent, yet simple, risk management model to implement.

- Accept no **unnecessary** risk.
- Accept risk when benefits outweigh cost.
- Make risk decisions at the right level.
- Anticipate and manage risk by planning.[1]

Situations also present the basis for developing and executing plans. As those plans are developed, OPSEC needs to be incorporated into the appropriate phases. Another acronym for mission planning, designed to keep things simple and concise is the SMEAC model. The purpose is to define the parameters of a particular mission in five paragraphs, with each letter identifying and describing the actions taken within the outlined phrase. The SMEAC format is used worldwide in both military and civilian applications. This is also known as the Five Paragraph Order, as it identifies the necessary components needed to carry out an order in a clear and easy to understand format.[2]

S - Situation
M - Mission
E - Execution
A - Administration/Logistics
C - Command/Signal

There are many variables to consider in each one of the planning paragraphs. These variables make it so where no two missions are exactly alike.

The SWOT method is another form of risk management tool. It is also referred to as an Internal-External Analysis and was developed in the 1960s by Albert S. Humphrey.[3] The acronym represents four key words focusing on the ability to identify potential risks. They are as follows:

S - Strengths
W - Weaknesses
O - Opportunities
T - Threats

This method requires objective, self-actualization and self-analysis and is better implemented when done as part of a team where they can evaluate and assess one another within the group.

"Be careful who you vent to; a listening ear can be a running mouth."
- Unknown

Citations:

[1] https://www.hvst.com/posts/risk-management-the-us-marine-corp-way-it-is-a-process-w8WTadG2
[2] https://en.wikipedia.org/wiki/Five_paragraph_order
[3] https://www.mindtools.com/pages/article/newTMC_05.htm

CHAPTER THREE

SURENESS or SUSPICION

"Trust not him with your secrets, who, when left alone in your room, turns over your papers."

— Johann Kaspar Lavater

Trust is the balancing point between the two extremes of sureness and suspicion. Any deviation from this point results in the scale tipping in either direction. Ideally, we would prefer the scale to tip towards sureness. However, this is a utopian pipe dream or happens with ten people, maybe less, during our entire lifetime. Our parents, siblings, and parents would be the most likely of persons to meet these criteria. Sadly, we know from personal experience or through watching the nightly news that even these people sometimes get more trust than they deserve. Therefore, we must accept the reality that some people will never earn our trust and be ever vigilant and watchful to those upon which we bestow our trust.

The four levels of trust I present in this book are based off the three-ringed circle of trust presented in a January 29, 2012 blog by Randy Conley entitled, *Leading with Trust*.[1] I have added an additional ring to include self; as there typically is a separation of trust, regardless of how healthy one believes it is to keep secrets from family members for whatever reason.

As such, I separate each level of trust into four categories: Self, Sanctum, Supporters, and Society. You can also see I have maintained my use of "S" words for the sake of continuity. The individual rings are not to scale or intended to be a measuring device determining how many people occupy any particular sector. While the popular "Circle of Trust" highlighted in the film, *Meet the Parents* is quite funny and holds some validity, the one presented here is far more accurate.

Would you be willing to trust this person without evaluating any of the potential risks? We must find the balance between paranoia and practicality in matters of trust. Photo courtesy of www.pixabay.com

Self - No one knows you better than you do. In all likelihood, there is probably no one else you trust more, either. Also included in this portion, is personal intuition and any attributable spiritual component. While I do not discount the notion of spiritual or supernatural assistance, most people are not compelled to accept this as a legitimate form of trust. It is entirely up to the reader to determine and assess its place within his or her circle of trust. However, solely relying on your own judgment puts you at greater risk. No single person can know everything, everybody, and the motives for every behavior displayed by others. Having the ability to seek advice and counsel from someone else helps aid in crucial decision-making.

Sanctum - Sanctum is for immediate family members and close, vetted friends with whom you have known for an established and appropriate length of time. Typically, there are only 2-10 individuals in this group.

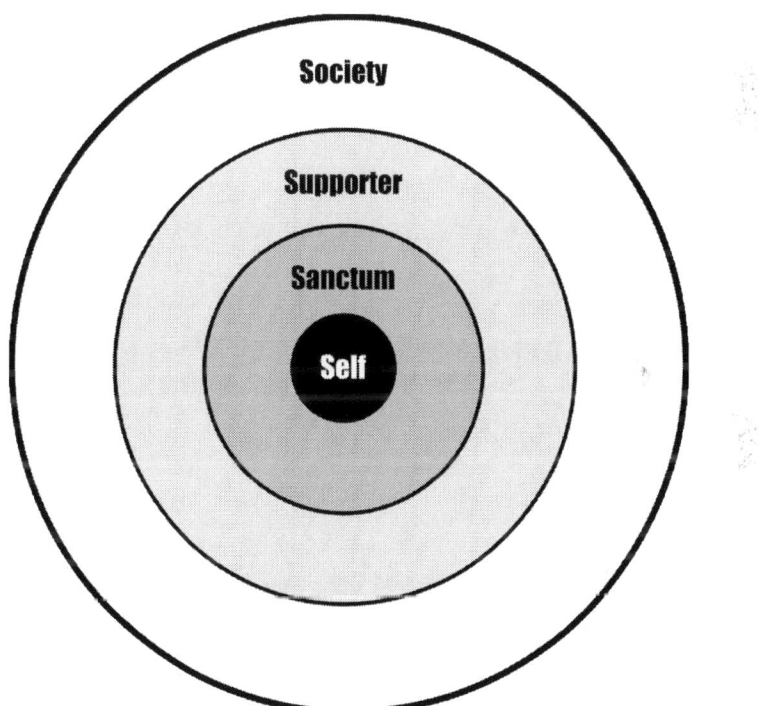

The circle of trust. Illustration by author.

Supporters - Supporters are acquaintances that have little knowledge of your everyday routine and schedules, but are generally supportive and often share several commonalities. This is where a majority of social media "friends" would typically appear. They can be members of the same organizations or clubs, cheer for the same sports team, or share the same political affiliation.

Society - Society is the generalized dumping ground for every other person whom you have no interaction or relationship. There may be individuals with whom you share common interests, but those interests do not necessarily warrant any unequivocal level of trust.

The outer circle of society can be divided further into three groups: Symbionts, Strangers, and Savages. This is illustrated in the next circle of trust model on the page 22.

Symbionts - Symbionts are those in society with whom you have an awareness of and provide a certain level of peaceful existence without having to have an immediately close relationship. By definition, these people are of a mutual benefit to you. An example would be those whom you have never met, but you all vote the same way and help create a group or majority to influence policy or the rest of society towards a held belief.

Strangers - These are the members of society whom you do not know. Their affiliations are not known to you, nor are their levels of assistance, ambivalence, or animosity towards you. This is a gray zone; so to speak, as members can migrate into other rings of the Society zone or even towards the inner zones of trust. The introduction to new people and friendship development are prime examples of this migration.

Savages - This group is obvious. These are the people whom you can reasonably assert, based on their held beliefs, and displayed behaviors that they are in direct opposition to you or your ideals and beliefs. They want to see you fail/cease to exist, or target their attacks towards you. They exist on the outer fringes of what your perception of society is because of these things. We actively try to avoid any contact with such people unless necessary or if there is a reasonable certainty allowing us to control the outcome in our favor.

It must be reiterated clearly, that in no way does the word savage imply, infer, or assert that certain people groups, ethnicities, cultures, or indigenous peoples are savages, completely or in part. Nor should the word be directly associated towards them. The threat of violence and general incivility of a person or persons against another is the common denominator to which the term is applied.

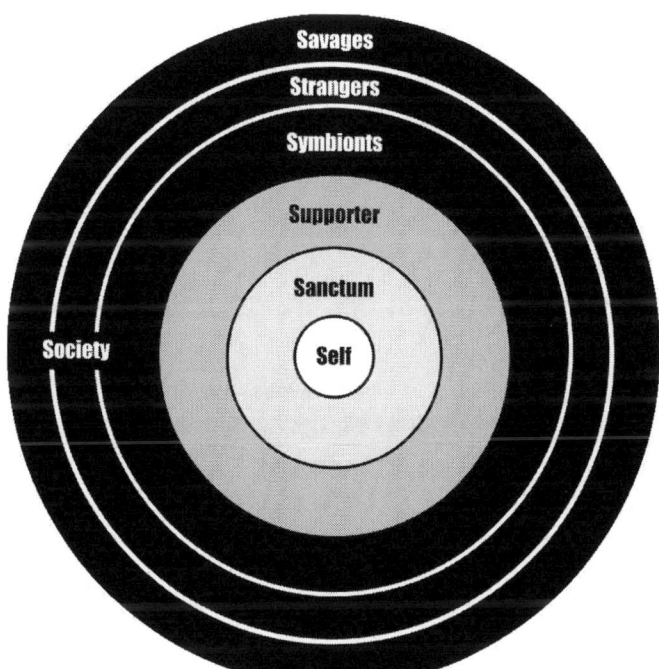

The three divisions within the society layer of the circle of trust. Illustration by author.

For context, let me share this example. Let us suppose I voted for Donald Trump instead of Hillary Clinton in the 2016 presidential election. Since the defeat, many Clinton supporters have been vocally upset regarding the election outcome. As a result, many Democrats have made numerous, hate-filled threats of ill will and violence towards conservatives, especially those who voted for and openly support Donald Trump. The countless tweets and other social media posts prove the existence of such threats and the stark irony of their hypocrisy in regards to their usual party platform rhetoric of tolerance and inclusion.

Those people, depending upon how true to their word they are, are a potential danger to me should my voting results become known to them. To be sure, there would be significant verbal abuse at the least, and everything in between leading up to physical assaults. With this knowledge and the propensity of undesirable conflict, I must decide carefully with whom I shall share this information. The question becomes, "Whom do I trust?"

Trust is at the very core of this work. No one likes to be on the receiving end of deceptive practices. However, most of us are not immune to falling victim to the many types of deception out there. Certain swindles are laughably detectable and easy to steer clear. Others are quite elaborate and complicated to spot. This is why it is called deception. No one comes right out and says, "I'm going to defraud you and embezzle money from you." Some personality types and demographics are more susceptible than other ones. We must carefully consider and acknowledge the tactics used to defraud others in order to avoid becoming victims ourselves.

The more we decide or allow ourselves to trust, the more vulnerable we become to having that trust violated. I am not advocating the position of "Trust no one...the world be damned" or whatever choice expletive you like and refuse to trust anyone. Doing so, however, is emotionally unhealthy and can imprison one in cell of loneliness, fear, and paranoia.

At the same time, we must also not be so naive as to think we are beyond fooling. Everyone has good and bad days. The longer we try to maintain a certain position of vigilance; we run the risk of becoming complacent if not given occasional reprieves.

Mitigating circumstances such as sleep deprivation, physical exhaustion, improper nutrition, and mental distractions all have negative effects on our ability to detect potential threats.

"Trust is like blood pressure. It's silent, vital to good health, and if abused, it can be deadly."

— **Frank Sonnenberg**

Citations:

[1]Conley, Randy, https://leadingwithtrust.com/2012/01/29/three-circles-of-trust/

CHAPTER FOUR

SECURITY

Reducing the amount of information, along with the type of information you share, is an added security benefit. Not only can it make you safer, but also those under your care and under your umbrella of responsibility. Ultimately, security is the desired goal. As security equals safety, it is understood that both should be pursued and maintained with great vigilance. Therefore, the sum sureness/suspicion you have of someone and the desired level of protection you desire will determine what security measures and the levels of security you choose to implement.

Just as security cameras are used to monitor locations and property, you must be equally vigilant. Photo courtesy of www.pixabay.com

There are several scenarios where protecting information becomes paramount. People, particularly we Americans, love to talk and speak our minds. After all, it is our right. We are proud of that right and we should be. However, if we want to keep what we value and ourselves safe, we need to know when, what, and where to tone it down a bit.

Unfortunately, one cannot slap a security label onto things and have it become instantly or impenetrably secure. We see security labeling everywhere around us. However, security in any of its manifestations is merely a deterrent. Its success in terms of prevention is subject to debate.

Security is only as good as the training received by the individuals providing the service. Security is a proactive measure requiring vigilance and frequent evaluation of procedures and protocols. Photo courtesy of www.pixabay.com

OPERATIONS SECURITY - Operations or Operational security (OPSEC) is a method of identifying crucial information and analyzing if the information and the actions/behaviors associated with it are observable to enemy intelligence.[1]

In a more general sense, OPSEC is like a jigsaw puzzle. Let us say you have a 1,000-piece puzzle. The overall puzzle may have a theme or "big picture", but within it, there may be a dozen or more objects or micro pictures. Each piece has the potential to display the aggregation, scale, or perspective of the overall subject. It is up to you (and others within your group, if applicable) to determine what pieces are mission essential and do not compromise plans or procedures pertaining to a mission.

Not all of our nation's cell phone networks are secure. This means all of our daily communications can be monitored, recorded, and archived. Photo courtesy of www.pixabay.com

PERSONAL SECURITY - Civilians often mistake personal security to mean operational security. PERSEC strictly pertains to an individual's personal information and his or her own physical safety and security. A person's Social Security number, Social media accounts, bank accounts, and medical records are examples of a part of PERSEC, just as door locks, security alarms, and self-defense weapons and training would be.

INFORMATION SECURITY - Information security (INFOSEC) is the practice of preventing unauthorized access, use, disclosure, disruption, modification, inspection, recording, or destruction of either electronic or physical information. Physical in this sense, would refer to paper or hard copy information on could physical hold, access, and view without the aid of computers or other piece of technology. The focus of all information security endeavors is a protection protocol that depends on the three elements of confidentiality, integrity, and availability of data.[2] Cyber security falls under the umbrella of information security as well and would include the protection of both hardware and software. As both of these have a monetary value, there is also an element of asset protection.

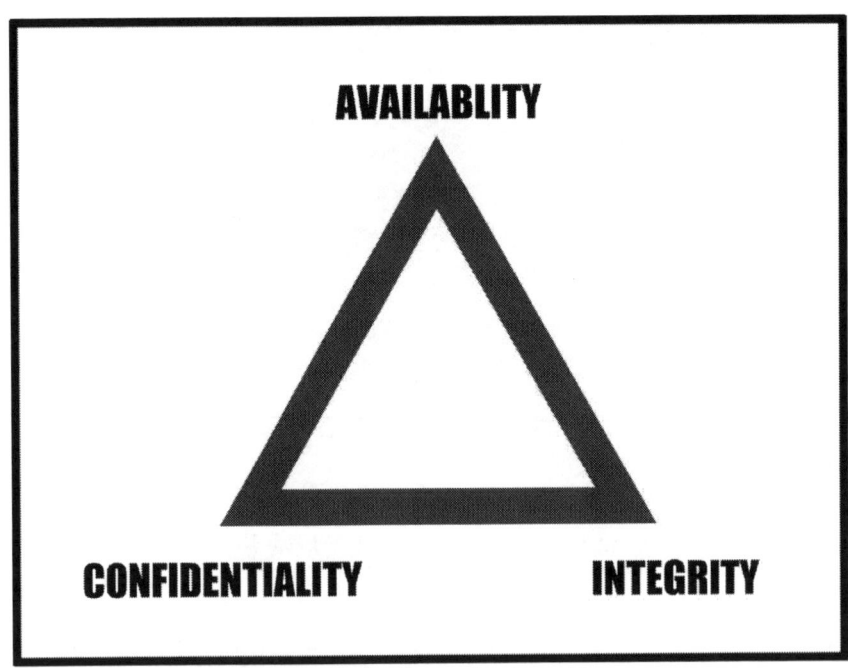

The CIA Triad. Illustration by author.

CIA TRIAD - This model displays the three crucial elements of protecting information from unwanted/unauthorized disclosure.

The triad is sometimes referred to as the AIC triad to avoid confusion or attributing its creation to the Central Intelligence Agency (CIA).[3]

"Trust, but verify."
- **Ronald Reagan**

Citations:

[1] https://en.wikipedia.org/wiki/Operations_security
[2] https://www.law.cornell.edu/uscode/text/44/3542
[3] https://whatis.techtarget.com/definition/Confidentiality-integrity-and-availability-CIA

SECTION II

Green Zone

CHAPTER FIVE

SIGNALING

Signaling has most of its behavioral roots in disciplines like body language, gestures, mannerisms, and their subsequent interpretations. This is where the concept of pretexting, or having planned responses for any number of contingencies that may arise when challenged by others. Challenging is a term often used to describe the purposeful, ordered confrontation of personnel who are attempting to gain access to a particular area. How we present ourselves when challenged can give away our true intentions subconsciously. The subconscious will be discussed later in Chapter 15.

Security guards and soldiers posted at the entrance gates to military bases are common examples. Once the proper credentials and/or identification are shown, the person is granted access. Those failing to meet those requirements are either turned away or detained in order verify their identity or ascertain the nature of their visit.

Signaling refers to more of the voluntary choice-driven behaviors we do. Sometimes, the signaling we present to others is intentional. These can include deliberate, "coded" actions that appear benign to a casual observer, but in fact, convey a covert message, which is only decipherable to the intended person who knows/possesses the key to decode the message.

The one example that comes to mind is the marking of a mailbox with a line of white chalk in the movie, *Enemy of the*

State, starring Gene Hackman and Will Smith. The premise is that no one would know how long the mark had been there, who put it there, or what it meant. It would likely wash off during the next rainstorm and because there is little or no symbolism associated with a single, random, straight line (other than the numeral 1) it is quickly dismissed by the casual observer. When drawn as diagonal line, it appears more like a check mark or a transfer from something scraping against it. The same thing can be achieved with a key, knife, or other metal object that can potentially scratch the surface and/or remove paint.

Hollywood obviously stylizes and exaggerates these types of signaling attempts in countless spy movies. There are also plenty of books, especially those discussing espionage during the Cold War between the United States and former United Soviet Socialist Republic (USSR).

How many times have you seen a similar scene in an espionage movie? Hollywood romantizes this type of locale for the dramatic elements offered within a film. What are some pros and cons to a meeting place such as this? Photo courtesy of www.pixabay.com

Oftentimes, the biggest contributor to our lack of success is directly linked to the amount of confidence we display. Showing signs of hesitation, timidity, or shiftiness will cause others to question and challenge our presence in a particular area. Dressing the part may help and feigning a little confusion to make conversational contact with someone might be of benefit as well. However, that confusion should only last long enough to bring the person over and then must take a back seat to confidence.

In addition to being very unhealthy, smoking can compromise surveillance efforts. However, in some countries, it provides an effective pretexting mechanism to establish contact with assets and targets. It's a bit clichéd, but it does work in some instances. Photo courtesy of www.pixabay.com

Signaling is the causation of all stimuli. It is the act of generating and transmitting signals, according to Collins Dictionary. While the term is most often used in economics and telecommunications, it does have a prevalent application in interpersonal communications.[1]

What makes signaling even more difficult to both control and comprehend is its inherent connection to the subconscious (discussed later in Chapter 15). Different countries and cultures may also have a pronounced distinction pertaining to the interpretation of any particular signal or body language behavior. Some body language meanings and gestures are very subtle and benign, while others can be polar opposite in certain cultures.

Citations:

[1]https://www.collinsdictionary.com/dictionary/english/signalling

CHAPTER SIX

SOCIAL SITES

Nothing in modern society has been more detrimental to secrecy and the concepts of OPSEC and PERSEC than the Internet. Millions and millions of people are enslaved to its power to generate revenue, conduct business, and connect people from around the world to personal workstations, home computers, and smartphones.

In the last decade, we have seen the result of data dumps onto the Internet by the likes of WikiLeaks founder Julian Assange and former CIA employee Edward Snowden. Regardless of whether you view these individuals as traitors or champions of the people, the consequences of the information released to the public have left both countries and political leaders vulnerable. Most of the inflicted damage has been at their own hands and well deserved, but releasing information just for the sake or releasing it is quite reckless.

Admittedly, I love it when the dirt and corruption of some politician or a hypocritical celebrity touting his devotion to socialism after he or she has made their gains from capitalism are exposed. Likewise, those who have differing political views enjoy it when those whom I support are caught.

While the argument exists and has a strong case of validity that it has made things easier, some believe it is not necessarily better. Facebook, the social media giant, is the modern-day Trojan Horse almost everyone carries in his or her hip pocket.

People, for some strange reason, have no problem sharing information, various pictures, personal opinion, etc. all over social media for their "friends" to see. My favorites are firearms owners, preppers, and survivalists who post pictures of everything from food supplies, ammunition supplies, and weapon arsenals. From an OPSEC standpoint, all I can do is shake my head and keep scrolling past. It does little good to tell people, so they will learn the hard way.

Years ago, it would take a surveillance team with a warrant to wire tap someone's phone in the hopes the person(s) of interest (POI) would make or receive a telephone call. Now, analysts monitor POI's social media accounts, if they have them. Then there were the mobile surveillance teams who spent hours trailing the POI to establish routines and contacts. These actions carried a significant risk of exposure or detection.

This is why it is potentially damaging or even dangerous to post too much information on social media. There are so many examples of the types of things you should not post on your social media pages, but oddly enough, people still do it. Companies and businesses are now starting to require non-disclosure agreements specifically to combat information leaks via social media. There is very little to help argue any claim you may make regarding permission or consent. There are people who have unintentionally, but willingly through the help of social media, lost their current job, ended their careers, or destroyed their political aspirations because they couldn't make the disconnect from their brains to their fingers.

Common Social Media Sites:

Facebook
Twitter

Instagram
Reddit
MySpace
Classmates
Tumblr
Yammer
Pinterest
Linked In
MyLife
Friendster
LiveJournal
YouTube
Snapchat
Facetime
Messenger
MeWe

Social media sites are a treasure trove of information about your interests, contacts, political affiliations, hobbies, family life, relationships, and more. Data miners and analysts exploit the information for targeted marketing and other nefarious purposes. Photo courtesy of www.pixabay.com

In the first half of 2018, Mark Zuckerberg, the founder of Facebook, appeared before a Congressional panel to explain allegations of data mining and content suppression.[1] While it may not cause a complete collapse of the social media giant, you can be sure that several thousands of people will close their accounts and use another.

To make matters worse, because Facebook offers the ability to create an account free of charge, means its intention is to both view and use account holders as a marketable product to third party advertisers. They analyze peoples' likes and affiliations to aid marketers to display their products toward their targeted demographic.

Internet use, specifically social media sites, needs to be kept to a minimum if one desires to protect one's privacy. Photo courtesy of www.pixabay.com

When Twitter was first introduced, it had a character limit for each tweet posted. This may have been done for a couple of legitimate reasons.[2] However; there may have been a few subversive ones that appear as a happy coincidence. On the subversive side, it is a form of suppression or restriction technique preventing people from saying anything while compiling or substantiating facts in a single tweet. Second, it fosters an atmosphere of poor grammar and spelling; people look for shortcuts, abbreviations, and acronyms to attempt to convey the majority of their message within the character limit parameters.

This, in turn, produces the third point of creating an intentional distortion of the context, allowing the content to be misunderstood or misconstrued. Creating misunderstanding in communication results in the creation of conflict. Lastly, the inclusion of multiple hash-tags (which once was known only as the pound symbol) fills one's newsfeed with every mention of any particular hash-tag. This fills the newsfeed with unrelated, irrelevant clutter. It's similar to transmitting a coded message along a noise/distortion filled carrier wave to hide the message.

Most of these social media sites do allow for some privacy. However, you have to take the initiative to turn on or off these features by often wading through a murky maze of menus and tabs in order to enjoy that increased privacy.

Citations:

[1] https://www.politico.com/story/2018/04/10/zuckerberg-senate-testimony-facebook-key-moments-512334
[2] https://www.quora.com/Why-does-Twitter-limit-the-message-length-to-140-characters

CHAPTER SEVEN

STRATEGIC SHARING

After going through all of these concepts, you may occasionally conclude that an individual or a group of individuals is worthy or in need of some crucial information sharing. Most of the time, we see what the procedure is for withholding information. If often transpires in scenarios with some official or politician holding a press conference. Anyone who has watched the news or watched a handful of spy movies is familiar with the non-committal phrase, "I can neither confirm nor deny that statement." All too often, this merely raises suspicion. At the very least, it acknowledges that some or no information has been sanitized for release to the public.

It should go without mentioning, that not all sharing of information is intended to be beneficial to the recipient or potential interceptors. Propaganda is a prime example of this tactic. This is also used to uncover moles or leaks within an intelligence community. Propaganda and misinformation have become so rampant over the past few years, that major media outlets and smaller, independent news agencies spend a great deal of time accusing one another of being a deliberate distributor of "fake news" or an accomplice to state-sponsored propaganda. Either way, the average citizen is at a loss and must devote considerable time and effort to find out the truth about what is being reported, and the why and how it's reported.

Propaganda is powerful, psychological tool used by governments and organizations to convince people of the virtue of a particular ideology. Photo courtesy of www.pixabay.com

In a discussion I once had with well-known combat tracking instructor, David Scott-Donelan, we were talking about the various roles of camouflage. When the subject gravitated to the stealth concept of sound, he mentioned that veiled or concealed speech is often known as propaganda. This conversation would be the catalyst for the book you have in your hand now.

The United States Marine Corps uses the acronym BAMCIS for establishing the sequence of events during a tactical operation. It's included here because of its relevant application to the topic and strategy development as a whole.[1]

B - Begin Planning
A - Arrange for Reconnaissance
M - Make Reconnaissance
C - Complete the Plan
I - Issue the Order
S - Supervise

However, there has been a circulating parody of this acronym, that while intended to poke fun at the concept of military intelligence and management, it does find a fitting context to the concepts of propaganda.

B - Begin the Lie
A - Arrange the Alibi
M - Make Excuses
C - Complete the Lie
I - Implicate Others
S - Shift the Blame

While making excuses and shifting the blame are components that good leaders and operatives should strive to avoid, I can visualize the context when these behaviors may be necessary in regards to propaganda and pretexting.

One of my favorite examples is the Navajo code talkers used during World War II. It was discovered that the Japanese had figured out how to intercept American transmissions. The United States promptly implemented the recruitment of Navajo Indians as radiomen to stop the intelligence breach and protect troop movements and maneuvers. Despite the interception of messages, the Japanese were never able to understand and decipher the Navajo language.[2]

Speech - Our everyday speaking voice, inflections, and tone give clear, concise meaning to the message communicated to others. This also includes the written language, in most instances. This is because of the crucial role of grammar and punctuation play in the understanding of context and intent of the message.

Slang - Slang can be regional or cultural words for various things or people that are not known or understood outside of the area where the word is commonly used. These words can often confuse people in regards to the context or the actual thing/person being discussed.

Even among different government agencies, information is often withheld. If/when, information is shared; it is done with regard to need to know, along with self-preservation for the releasing agency. Photo courtesy of www.pixabay.com

Syntax - Syntax involves some of the more confusing intricacies of the English language (and probably several other languages, too) such as homonyms, homophones, and homographs. Homonyms are words that either are pronounced or spelled the same as another word, while having different meanings. Homophones are words that sound the same, but have different meanings and spelling. Homographs are words spelled exactly the same, but have different meanings and pronunciation.

Slander - Slander is the intentional use of spoken words within the public arena to publically discredit, malign, or damage another person's business or reputation. The key emphasis being that which is spoken is untrue or a lie. Slander is not protected in any such way and can have serious civil and criminal implications. This is discussed in the next chapter on Suppression.

"Don't trust people who tell you other people's secrets."

- Dan Howell

Citations:

[1]https://www.trngcmd.marines.mil/Portals/207/Docs/TBS/B2B23 67%20Tactical%20Planning.pdf, page 5
[2]https://www.cia.gov/news-information/featured-story-archive/ 2008-featured-story-archive/navajo-code-talkers/

SECTION III

Yellow Zone

CHAPTER EIGHT

SUPPRESSION

Suppression is the word I use often to describe self-imposed censorship. Censorship is a hot topic these days, with both major political parties claiming to be victim at the hands of the other. Unfortunately, too many Americans have a poor understanding of what is exactly written in the US Constitution. Their knowledge of individual rights begins and ends with the First Amendment. After that, the concept of how and why we attempt to preserve and protect those rights becomes a point of great contention and debate.

Censorship has always been a hot topic in America, even before the Declaration of Independence and the U.S. Constitution were written. Photo courtesy of www.pixabay.com

"Congress shall make no law respecting an establishment of religion, or prohibiting the free exercise thereof; or abridging the freedom of speech, or of the press; or the right of the people peaceably to assemble, and to petition the Government for a redress of grievances."[1]

- First Amendment of Article I of the United States Constitution

Whenever the topic of censorship is brought up, "Freedom of speech" is always the retaliatory battle cry. Unfortunately, in this day and age, many people seem to think freedom of speech is exempt from consequences. These same people also hold the belief that having an opinion automatically grants them an audience, regardless of the tolerance or preference of that audience. To make matters worse, the Constitutional illiteracy displayed by protestors is the epitome of irony and hypocrisy. Hundreds and thousands gather in the name of the latest social cause demanding the rights of others be sanctioned, restricted, or altogether removed; only to unknowingly trample and threaten their own inherit rights. It is to this end that many are unaware; that their rights end exactly at the point where they infringe or threaten someone else's rights.

To exacerbate the problem further, many Americans lack the fundamental understanding of how legal precedence affects what we say and how we say it. Nor do they understand, in legal terms, what *fighting words* are, what *slander* is, and why you cannot use the freedom of speech as an excuse to incite violence or panic in public places and in society as a whole.

The Merriam-Webster dictionary website defines fighting words as "words which by their very utterance are likely to inflict harm on or provoke a breach of the peace by the average person to whom they are directed." [2] As a result of the Supreme Court (SCOTUS) ruling in 1942 regarding Chaplinsky v New Hampshire, 315 U.S. 568, fighting words are not protected speech under the First Amendment to the U.S. Constitution.[3]

The recent protests regarding the unfortunate school shooting at Parkland Ridge high school in Florida uncovers just how unknowledgeable the public are when it comes to a discussion about rights. The government does not grant rights. The role of government is to protect and secure the rights endowed upon us by our Creator.

There are people and governments that data mine your personal information for various reasons ranging from nuisance privacy invasion to malicious identity theft. Photo courtesy of www.pixabay.com

Government agencies, military forces, and even private citizens need to re-embrace the concept of privileged information and withholding it from the public or anyone else who does not have a valid, operational need-to-know. Nowhere in the First

Amendment, when speaking about the freedom of the press, does it state or allude to an acknowledgement of the public's right to know. Nor does it grant *carte blanche* dissemination of that information

In the same manner, few people are compelled to share every private detail of their life and share it with millions of other people. Nobody openly gives out his or her Social Security number or his or her bank account information. Why? Generally speaking, people cannot be trusted (and should not) to not use the information in an illegal or fraudulent manner.

"Trust no one; tell your secrets to nobody and no one will ever betray you."
- Bigvai Volcy

Suppression is similar to what we would call "sanitizing" in the military. Before anyone who didn't possess the proper clearance or valid need-to-know could enter a secure communications area, we would "sanitize" the area. This entailed removing any classified material from desktops, computer screens, etc. and securing those items in closed and locked cabinets. Any equipment too large or impractical to remove was covered up with sheets or blocked off with curtains or partitions. Everywhere the individual worked and the pathways to and from those spaces would be free of any classified information and there were to be no discussions within earshot or the uncleared visitor.

This is often done to accommodate building contractors who have clearance and authority to maintain a building, but don't have a security clearance. It would be impractical to issue a security clearance in these types of situations. During their time in these areas, an escort by someone with the necessary security clearance would be with the individual at all times.

Citations:

[1] https://en.wikipedia.org/wiki/First_Amendment_to_the_United_States_Constitution
[2] https://www.merriam-webster.com/legal/fighting%20words
[3] https://www.law.cornell.edu/wex/fighting_words

CHAPTER NINE

SELECTIVITY

"Whoever is careless with the truth in small matters cannot be trusted with important matters."

— **Albert Einstein**

In the Navy, and the military in general, regarding the disseminating of information, it came down to two components: appropriate security clearance and possessing/articulating a valid need to know. Oftentimes, only one qualifier was met. This was usually the clearance portion, as most people within the building had to have security clearance just to gain access into and work in the building.

Demonstrating the second portion, the valid need to know, was selective and very circumstantial. Not only did the circumstances dictate access, but also the immediacy of use had to be determined and justified. I have several friends who work or have worked in government agencies, as government contractors, general military, special operations (SPEC OP) groups, police departments, etc.

However, those established friendships don't entitle me, in any way, to any of the classified information they may possess. When I interview or call them up regarding certain topics, they allow for some general speculation on my part, and may give a confirming nod if I'm on the right path, buy they can't volunteer any specific information.

These two components are often the best rule of thumb when determining selectivity of who is to be the recipient of any valuable information or plans you intend to share. The system is not foolproof and not without the risk of circumvention, but it is a model for the everyday person to use. Now, it is obvious that you would not (and probably could not) issue a security card to every person you know and trust with certain aspects of your personal lives. Despite this, you should be able to create a list of trustworthy individuals that you choose to grant access to information. The issuance of cards appears professional and efficient, but just like any other physical item; they are susceptible to being misplaced, lost, or stolen.

Information loss. Illustration by author.

It used to be that way with your issued Social Security card. Only you were supposed to know your number. Now, however, employers, numerous government agencies, financial institutions, universities, all have it on record or access to it. Of course, the IRS (Internal Revenue Service) has it as well. In the age of on-demand information and lightning fast information retrieval, it is no wonder the system has been compromised and exploited by hackers.

Examine the previous illustration. The barrel contains the information that you want to safeguard. There are four ways the information can be compromised. You can observe another series of "S" words is used to discuss and describe information loss and disclosure. Over time, the storage method can deteriorate and no longer provide the necessary security. Unintended compromises would be seepage and spills; however, it doesn't *always* mean that the information loss is accidental. All four can be the result of sabotage.

In an effort to clean up spills and seepage, sponging refers to the absorption of information, which may then be returned to a proper storage facility/container or secretly collected with the intention of it removal for unauthorized dissemination. Siphoning is often construed as deliberate and intentional. Just as someone would siphon fuel from a vehicle, it is reasonably suggested that the intent is criminal, or at the very least, suspicious.

Another aspect of selectivity to consider is words. The words we use every day in both written and oratory formats can alter the meaning of the intended message. This alludes back to Chapter 7 when discussing speech, slang, syntax, and slander. In order to have an effective code language between two parties is a valid, matching cipher and corresponding decoding key. If the two items don't match, messages come across as a garbled mess of unreadable text.

Selectivity provides options for who gains access and what information is present behind certain access points. This is the concept of compartmentalization Photo courtesy of www.pixabay.com

In the Navy, each command, whether ship or shore installation, has a CMS (Communication Security Material) Coordinator who oversees the issuance of the ciphers and the loading methods/devices used to update the crypto portions of communications systems, according to Naval Operation Instructions (OPNAV) and a whole slew of other three-letter acronym agencies like DOD, DIA, and NSA.

Safeguarding secrets is a big deal and it's an even bigger deal when secrets are compromised, whether by accidental carelessness or by intentional acts of treason. When you have something of value or is valuable exclusively to you or a select few around you, you take whatever precautions and steps to ensure the safety and protection of those things. Even at the risk of offending or ostracizing someone else who hasn't met your requirements of trust, you must be willing to incorporate safeguards.

My wife and I instituted the use of passwords with our daughters from a young age. As soon as they we able, we introduced them to the concept of verbal ciphers to distinguish against friends and strangers. No adult, caregiver, or family friend would be allowed to take our children anywhere in our absence without verbally verifying the chosen password with the girls. If the password was incorrect, they stay put. Fortunately, we have never had to follow up with secondary responses or rapid evacuations because one of us is always present to pick up the girls from school or take them where they need to go.

"Keep your friends close, but your enemies closer."

- Michael Corleone, *The Godfather Part II*

One of the more provocative measures used by any number of agenda-based advocacy groups, political parties, social justice warriors, and conspiracy theorists these days is a form of selectivity called contextomy. Matthew McGlone of the University of Texas at Austin stated this academic term describes the intentional selection of excerpted words or phrases from its "original linguistic context in a way that distorts the source's intended meaning". Most people refer to this as taking a quote out of context. McGlone goes on to say the practice encourages the hearer(s) to form misinformed/ill-informed opinions of the original intention or bias further interpretation when re-introduced to the original context.[1]

Politicians are particularly fond of this tactic to defame political opponents, sidestep allegations, and defend their position on controversial issues. By selecting a portion of a question to answer and elaborate on the trivials, they effectively avoid the question while still appearing to provide a response.

Selectivity can also describe the use of codes and ciphers. The biggest drawback, next to a compromise of the cipher and the key, is that its implementation requires agreement from both the receiver and the sender; meaning both parties must have the correct code and key in order to transmit accurate messages. A famous example is the phrase "One if by land, two if by sea." to describe the events of April 18, 1775, when Paul Revere warned colonists of the impending British invasion. While this was the agreed upon code, the eloquence of the phrase is actually from the poem, *Paul Revere's Ride* by Henry Wadsworth Longfellow, written some 80 years after the event took place.[2]

"Do not tell secrets to those whose faith and silence you have not already tested.
- **Queen Elizabeth I**

Citations:

[1] https://techcrunch.com/2014/02/14/how-the-world-butchered-benjamin-franklins-quote-on-liberty-vs-security/
[2] http://oldnorth.com/historic-site/the-events-of-april-18-1775/

CHAPTER TEN

SCRUTINY

Scrutiny has definite, harsh underpinnings associated with its meaning and application. It does not sit well with people who fantasize about or have a dedication to utopian harmony. It is the polar opposite of inclusiveness and teamwork, unequivocal trust and non-biased behavior.

To be frank, scrutiny is the proverbial endoscopy used by others charged with finding out what's inside of someone by either of the two available/accessible orifices. It's not pleasant, but is often the means in which people are vetted for access to highly sensitive or classified material and information.

I remember the nervousness I felt when interviewed for my naval security clearance. I recall the uncomfortable tension of being subjected to a polygraph for an armored car company I worked for a couple of years. I distinctly disliked the mental probing by the psychologist when applying for a Department of Corrections job. All of these things are necessary to determine another S word, *suitability*. Are you suitable to be granted the access, the authority, and to accept the accountability of which the position entails?

Scrutiny can be established by the introduction to code words or phrases. However, codes and code words can be a double-edged sword. Long periods of infrequent use make remembering certain situational code words or phrases difficult.

Adding factors such as sleep deprivation, malnutrition, and duress caused by injury or stress often derails their effectiveness.

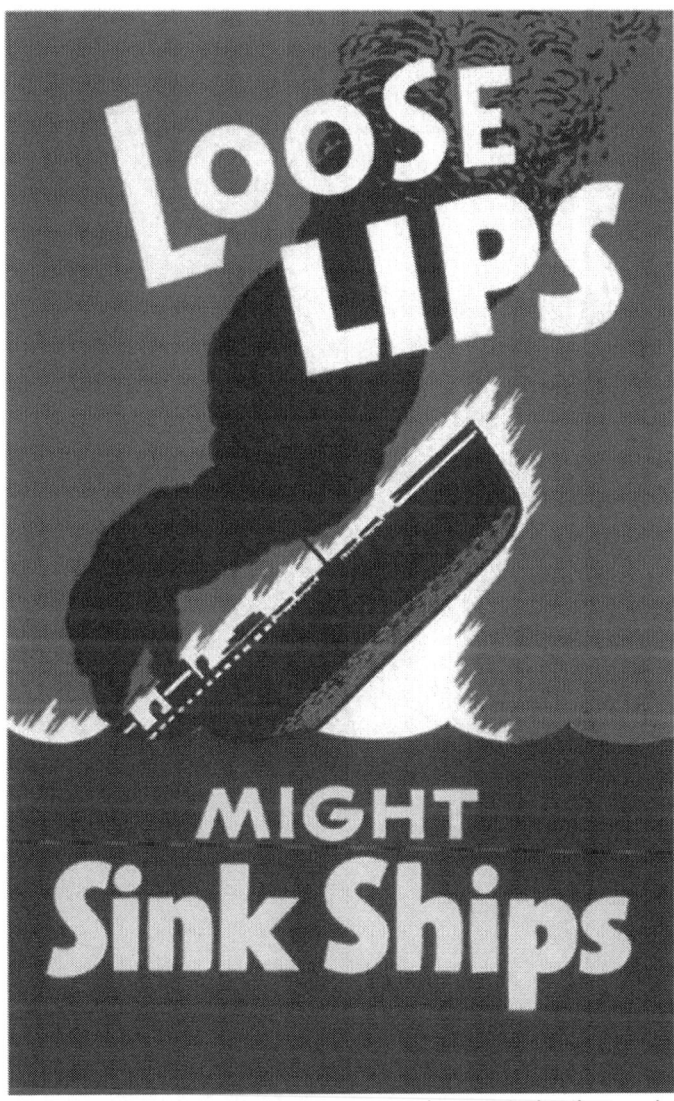

World War II era posters like this one were used to remind sailors and Marines about the dangers of talking about ships' movements while in liberty ports and when writing letters back home.

On the opposite end of the spectrum, overuse of code words and phrases run the risk of compromise and exposure to unauthorized persons. When I was in the Navy, we would change the cipher key every month. Frequent code-word changes help facilitate an effective security protocol.

"There are two rules for success: 1) Never tell everything you know."

- Roger H. Lincoln

A good basic introduction into the use of code words is to look at the example of the phonetic alphabet. Anyone with previous military experience or law enforcement/first responder service will be familiar with this system of communication. This is extensively used by all member countries of the North Atlantic Treaty Organization (NATO). As English is the primary international language used, the phonetic alphabet is intended to overcome and eliminate the confusion of the letters B, C, D, E, G, P, T, V, and Z. These letters have the tendency to sound similar when spoken too fast, spoken with heavy accents and dialects, or with certain speech impediments.

The NATO Phonetic Alphabet:

A - Alpha
B - Bravo
C - Charlie
D - Delta
E - Echo
F - Foxtrot
G - Golf
H - Hotel
I - India
J - Juliet

L - Lima
M - Mike
N - November
O - Oscar
P - Papa
Q - Quebec
R - Romeo
S - Sierra
T - Tango
U - Uniform
V - Victor
W - Whiskey
X - X-Ray
Y - Yankee
Z - Zulu

Naturally, the average civilian may not know this, which makes it easier for military, police, security personnel, and bodyguards to spell out code names, locations, call signs, etc. without the general public knowing what is been spoken. This protects the names of people under executive protection, as well as the identities of police and security units.

"Trust is built with consistency."

- Lincoln Chafee

CHAPTER ELEVEN

SIGNIFICANCE

Anything that appears out of the ordinary or contrary to a recognized, set routine is significant. Significance is so important, that it is a word commonly used by police when taking witness reports and investigations. They want information that stands out. They want glaring differences, while at the same time, desiring commonalities or agreement between witness statements. This is often referred to as corroborating evidence or statements. Facts, although obtained from two different sources or individuals, support and validate the statement made by another.

In the seemingly endless stream of commonality, there are those seeking to zero in on anything significant. Photo courtesy of www.pixabay.com

The search for significance is so compelling among intelligence agencies and federal law enforcement agencies that computer algorithms are created to find even the smallest of irregularities or identifying features. You are probably more familiar with its practice through Internet search engines that use search engine optimization (SEO), meta-word, and keyword searches to rapidly retrieve information similar to the topic typed in the search box.

Monitoring/surveillance equipment is highly mobile and portable; reaching the point of being executed effectively with a Smartphone, rather than a high-tech set-up similar to the one pictured here. Photo courtesy of www.pixabay.com

I often imagine what it must look like in the deep confines of our nation's intelligence community. There must be endless corridors of computers collecting and analyzing terabyte after terabyte of data, all to detect anomalies posing a possible threat to our national security. There must be several hundred terminals and workstations with a similar appearance to the high-tech surveillance and information systems used by Bruce Wayne as he masquerades as the winged vigilante, Batman, in comic books.

Tattoos are a prime example. The cultural acceptance of tattoos has increased considerably, even to the point of becoming fad in some parts of the country. In decades past, the number of people having tattoos was less and those who were tattooed were often belonging to certain portions of society. I can appreciate the artistic expression of tattoos, but they often become a strong identifier, especially if the artwork or theme of the tattoo is unique. Other personal attributes, which are uncontrollable or extremely difficult to alter, can be significant if we find ourselves falling into the search parameters.

Significance Indicators

If you recall back in Chapter 4 discussing about OPSEC, the term aggregation appeared and I likened it to a jigsaw puzzle. All of the individual pieces give potential clues as to the types of activities you may not wish to broadcast. Here are some factors that may or may not be significant by themselves, but help form theories or conclusions that can later compromise your security and put yourself or your group at risk.

- Time
- Date
- Location
- Duration
- Activity
- Members/people involved
- Pre-/Post-event communications
- Equipment used
- Attire
- Attitude/Morale

These ten significance indicators can be pieced together to draw conclusions about possible plans or activities. Not only would such things indicate your plans, but also allows an enemy to examine a potential time to ambush you or your group while key members are focused on some other matter. A longer observation time will generate more INTEL. Look at the letters of the alphabet below. You can see a great number of significance indicators. There are variations, some only using one indicator per letter. However, it is a useful technique used by police and military units to identify high value targets (HVTs) or suspects.

A - Age, Activity, Address, Associates, Aliases, Accent, Alarms
B - Build, Behavior, Buildings
C - Color, Complexion, Communications, Clothes, Characteristics
D - Demeanor, Duration, Dates, Defenses, Dedication, Dexterity
E - Eyes, Equipment, Entry/Exits, Ethnicity
F - Family, Foes, Friends, Firearms, Facial Features, Fanatic
G - Gear, Gait, Glasses, Gangs, Groups, Gender, Guards
H - Hierarchy, Habits, Height, Hair
I - Itineraries, Intentions, Intelligence, Identities, Internet
J - Jewelry, Jobs, Jurisdiction
K - Kits, Kids, Knowledge
L - Location, Language, Livestock, Landscape, Leadership
M - Mannerisms, Movements, Marks, Motives, Money
N - Narcotics, Novice, News
O - Occupation, Orientation, Operations, Observation
P - Plans, Projects, Personnel, Priorities, Professional
Q - Quantities, Qualities
R - Race, Routes, Routines, Record
S - Sex, Speech, Scars, Strengths, Supplies, Structures, Sentries
T - Tactics, Tattoos, Training, Technology, Times, Terrain
U - Utilities, Unknowns
V - Vices, Vehicles, VIPs, Vigilance, Violence
W - Weight, Weapons, Weaknesses

X - X-ceptions, X-perts, X-perience
Y - Youth
Z - Zeal, Zones, Zoology

There is always a possibility of being observed without your knowledge. Your behavior determines what information they can assert or assume. Photo courtesy of www.pixabay.com

These are just some of the possible things that can be observed and provide a lot of information. Some of them are possibly repeated in order to present a different angle regarding a particular aspect. For instance, you may know a person's occupation from another intelligence source, but it is not the job he/she is currently doing while under observation. As I mentioned before, the more time a surveillance team has to monitor a target, the more of these significance indicators go from being unknown to known.

For example, your survival group is planning to scout out the nearby town in search of supplies. Unbeknownst to your group, a two-man scout team has been able to monitor your base camp for the last week. They know how many people are in the camp, with a specific breakdown of men, women, and children. They observe meal times; watch rotations, and meeting times.

They know where surplus weapons and supplies are held and who normally is carrying weapons. The sentry positions are known to them and which sentries are vulnerable due to inexperience or complacency. They observe and record the communications protocol of the sentries and how they report events, use code-words, hand signals, and call signs.

The day your reconnaissance group is to leave, the hostile scout team observes the packs and extra ammunition taken by the five-man team. The scouts are able to determine which of the departing five-man team has prior military experience or training and has established the chain of command within that team and the camp itself.

SECTION IV

Red Zone

CHAPTER TWELVE

SILENCE

Many have heard it said that nothing is more deafening than silence. Silence makes most people uncomfortable; even to the point of starting awkward conversations with frivolous talking points just to make the silence cease.

Silence is often the best option, but not the most practical. Our everyday lives require a certain level of communication through speech and body language to engage in necessary conversations with others. Photo courtesy of www.pixabay.com

Because of this notion, many interviewers, investigators, and interrogators employ this tactic to passively manipulate subjects into divulging more information than what the subject should or want; without having to rely on ways that can be articulated or described as forced.

"We have two ears and one mouth so that we can listen twice as much as we speak."

- Epictetus

This is especially important for people who consciously or subconsciously talk to themselves or talk aloud with no specific audience. Silence or the deliberate reduction in speaking volume is not always a foolproof way to keep out invasive ears. The sensory organs of the human body work together to piece together all types of information to complete the "puzzle" the individual has on task.

If you are like many people, you perhaps glanced at the back cover of the book prior to purchasing. You will notice that at the end of the last paragraph, I mention the most important "S" word regarding OPSEC, the word "*Shhh*."

Silence is often viewed as the antithesis to speaking. However, it does not entirely end or cause the intended breakdown in communication. Once our oral language has stopped, the other person(s) intent on maintaining the flow of communication must troubleshoot the disruption of the transmission and determine the cause.

It was once believed (and still is) that refusing to speak was considered a sign of guilt. Police investigators still use this ingrained belief to coerce suspects to waive their rights and subversively coax confessions from them when there is no physical evidence linking the suspect to the crime. It is a dirty, under-handed tactic and unconstitutional, yet, it still happens.

This type of underhanded behavior is now the reason police are now required to "read people their rights" at the time of an arrest. This goes back to a 1966 Supreme Court case, *Miranda v. Arizona*, 384 U.S. 436, in which a suspect's confession was not admissible in court because he did not know his rights, was not made aware that he had rights that protected him from self-incrimination and access to an attorney prior to questioning.[1] While it did not reverse Miranda's conviction, the ruling by the Supreme Court did, in fact, change arrest and interrogation procedures nationwide as a result.

The darker side of silence comes at a painful cost for some. The reality is that people, regimes, and governments have used less than humane methods to receive intelligence and information. This statement and the following commentary on this subject is merely an acknowledgement of its existence and use, not an advocating or condoning of such behavior.

The prospect of torture is a frightening scenario. Less invasive forms such as isolation start the lower levels and progress to severe physical and psychological abuses. Photo courtesy of www.pixabay.com

Countless prisoners of war (POWs) and even suspects held by police have been tortured to gain information or to extract a coerced confession under duress. The practice, while extremely violent and deemed unethical in our modern times, was often a tactic used, not only to procure intelligence regarding an enemy force, but also used as a deterrent to keep citizenry in line. Citizens dared not break from the demanding conformity offered by rulers. Doing so resulted in swift, painful, and often permanent reminders that disobedience would not be tolerated.

Despite what is often presented in movies and novels, no one on the receiving end of torture welcomes the suffering with taunts and machismo. It is frightening, painful, and leaves one demoralized, undignified, and physically and emotionally scarred. This is why there is a strong emphasis on Survival, Evasion, Resistance, Escape (SERE) training. Course instructors "break" every student. Everyone has a breaking point regarding what they can endure both physically and mentally.

"Everybody breaks! That's the point! Damn thing doesn't stop till you break."

- Walter Burke, *The Recruit*

This hopefully reinforces the desire within students to avoid capture in the first place. From a mission standpoint, all remaining team members will or should assume that the mission is now compromised, as enemy forces will immediately begin extracting any intelligence that they can. While I'm not going to present types or methods in depth, I will state that there are often three tiers or levels used during enhanced interrogations.

The first level is used to establish a baseline of truth from the individual. Depending on the time constraints of the captors, they initially may use isolation and depravation techniques to lower the morale. The second level is much more focused and intense, introducing pain and physical discomfort to further lower and break the morale. The third level involves the introduction of the peacemaker or deal broker. They come in offering alleviation from the suffering in return for the information they want or further information. It should be no surprise that freedom or release comes in the common form of execution. Most Westernized countries refrain from negotiating with terrorists or drug cartels holding hostages; rescues are never a sure bet. As such, the best strategy lies in not being captured at all.

While the possibility exists of gaining some counter-intelligence information, the practice of subjecting oneself to enhanced interrogation methods strictly for that purpose is both foolish and dangerous. The mind can only suffer so much before losing consciousness or tries to repress or suppress the experience through mental avoidance techniques. Furthermore, the psychological impact of such an ordeal may require intense counseling or therapy to overcome the trauma. It is better to avoid capture or situations where your physical and mental capabilities are exploited and abused for the purpose of acquiring the information you possess.

As mentioned earlier, everyone has personal breaking limits. Fear and the certainty of discomfort are powerful tools, so don't ever think or assume that you'll be able to hold out until a rescue comes. Physiological response and phobias will expose your weaknesses long before any rescuer will show up. I can promise you of that fact.

Citations:

[1] http://www.uscourts.gov/educational-resources/educational-activities/facts-and-case-summary-miranda-v-arizona

CHAPTER THIRTEEN

SECRETS

Everyone has secrets. A secret is information about a person, thing, place, subject, or idea that its creator or possessor intends to withhold from others. The reason for the withholding can be equally varied ranging from the benign, such as a surprise birthday party, to the malignant and criminal, like the murder of a political opponent to assure an election victory.

While the exact reasons for initiating or maintaining a secret vary, the common factor for both is some form of protection. This could be personal protection for some. It may be asset protection or the securing of proprietary information to prevent competitors from gaining access to product designs, material composition, and operational specifications.

The litmus test for a secret is the amount of damage or consequences that occur as a result of a disclosure or compromise of that secret. For instance, if a man buys a gift for his wife, intending it to be a secret until a particular time or place, it's not really a secret. If he tells her or gives the gift early, he merely has a problem of being able to control his excitement along with his outward expression of his love for his wife. Neither of which will cause damage to his relationship.

However, let's assume he makes the money used to buy the gift selling drugs or some other equally reprehensible act in the eyes of his spouse. What are the possible consequences if the means in which he procured the funds comes into light?

I remember watching the Steven Seagal action movie, *Above the Law*, and being shocked to see a government compartmentalization code word shown on-screen. It was not one of those quick, Hollywood "Easter Eggs" for fans to find. It was obvious. The National Security Agency (NSA) still uses the word internally for Communications Intelligence (COMINT).[1] While documents routinely become de-classified; I am still not in the habit of disclosing that type of information, especially for the sake of Hollywood realism.

Although replaced by the advancements of technology, the miniature spy camera was once a main staple of those engaged in the dangerous art of espionage. Photo courtesy of www.pixabay.com

The old line from *Top Gun*, "It's classified...I could tell you, but then I'd have to kill you," is also the stuff of Hollywood. If someone in the military intentionally disseminates classified information, they are arrested, indicted, convicted, and finally sentenced to a military prison stay in Ft. Leavenworth, in Kansas. However, in the recent 2016 election cycles, releasing classified emails and the subsequent deletion thereof, failed to produce either an indictment or conviction of one particular candidate. I can assure you that this was an extreme exception and not the norm. Many have served extensive prison terms for actions that were far less egregious in both face value and actual damage. However, I digress.

If the security breach is egregious enough, the only deaths are those of embedded foreign operatives whose identity has been compromised or the traitor who leaked the information at the hands of the executioner. We often want the latter to be the only casualty, but it is often not the reality.

There is also the component that often fuels the fires of countless conspiracy theories. Some people are so driven to protect information, their reputations, and their behavior out of the public eye, that they, in fact, do commit murder or use the tactics of threats of violence, intimidation, and extortion to prevent disclosure.

We see these types of accusations hurled predominantly towards political figures. There are even websites and online sources that gather lists of mysterious deaths, accidents, and questionable suicides of individuals who have met with an untimely death soon after they revealed damning knowledge of someone or just before they were to testify. The most notable ones often involve members of the Clinton family, the most famous being the "Clinton Body Count".[2]

As often as the accusations seem reasonable and viable, our court systems do not recognize coincidence and circumstantial evidence as having precedent over confirmed fact and physical evidence. I personally would find some satisfaction if certain political figures could be brought to justice using this information, however, it then becomes a potentially slippery slope in which everyone subject to the justice system were to be evaluated and scrutinized the same way.

"Three can keep a secret, if two of them are dead."

- Benjamin Franklin

Citations:

[1]https://electrospaces.blogspot.com.au/2014/07/nsa-still-uses-umbra-compartment-for.html
[2]http://www.slate.com/articles/news_and_politics/explainer/1999/02/does_bill_clinton_run_murder_inc.html

CHAPTER FOURTEEN

SUBTERFUGE

Subterfuge isn't a commonly used word today, but most people recognize it by definition. It is the act of lying or purposely engaging in the practice of deception. One of the biggest conscious struggles is the stigma produced by these practices. There have been plenty of theses, manuscripts, and religious texts dedicated to this topic. It is my hope that most people reading this book also have had the added benefit of a parent(s) or an authority figure that instilled the values of integrity and trustworthiness. However, in the future, the need to incorporate a little deception to keep you, your family, your group, or even your church safe, may require you to deceive someone out to do you harm.

This usually means people need to find a comfortable middle ground between sainthood and being sinister. I know... more "S" words. It should be noted that a major tenet of Islam is the practice of *taqiyya*. It provides a follower of Islam the permission to deceive a non-believer or infidel for the purpose of self-preservation and/or the furtherance of Islam.[1] Al-Taqiyya is literally defined as the "concealing or disguising one's beliefs, convictions, ideas, feelings, opinions, and/or strategies at a time of eminent danger, whether now or later in time, to save oneself from physical and/or mental injury."[2]

While the two major sects of Islam dispute its use, both sects have writings devoted to the subject and acknowledge its existence. This brings up a major concern for Westerners and practitioners of other religions, as it would drastically affect one's ability to establish a relationship or partnership with one participant having deity-granted permission and approval to lie and deceive the other. The question then becomes why anyone would willfully choose to enter into any type of business agreement, partnership, or even a treaty with any party whom you could not trust.

Unfortunately, the followers of Islam have brought this upon themselves, having no one else to blame for the general distrust directed towards them. Because the directive exists in their written texts, there is no point in denying its existence. As they have no avenue of discourse against the Quran and the Hadith; their stubborn refusal to work towards a meaningful reformation that would incorporate modern world views regarding the subjects of slavery, women's rights, and assimilation into Western society, does little to help generate sympathy towards its' followers. Christians are often accused of the same level of bigotry and hypocrisy because Christ Himself instructed His followers "to be perfect."[3] Hence, anytime a Christian fails to meet the standard of perfection set forth by Christ's example, there is bound to be someone to point it out.

This may not mean that Muslims are incapable of or have no desire whatsoever to be truthful with people of differing faiths. However, it is an incredibly large hurdle to overcome. Especially, among people who can only see the potential of taqiyya being practiced through limited and isolated study of excerpts and texts. There are plenty of examples within the Old Testament of the Holy Bible where people did the same thing. They lied and/or withheld information to protect themselves or someone else. Moreover, while these examples exist, there isn't a specific passage of scripture giving permission to do so from God, in the

Ten Commandments or any elaboration or assertion in the Levitical Code.

"In war-time, truth is so precious that she should always be attended by a bodyguard of lies."
- **Winston Churchill**

Wartime is not the only time to put this concept into practice. The deliberate omission of truth is often necessary for our survival. One could hardly expect Jews during World War II to admit openly their heritage, knowing that the Nazis wanted to send them to concentration camps and later exterminate them. Anyone placed in a similar circumstance would lie or withhold information to protect themselves and their loved ones. To display another type of behavior would show a distinct and unnatural lack of self-preservation and apathy.

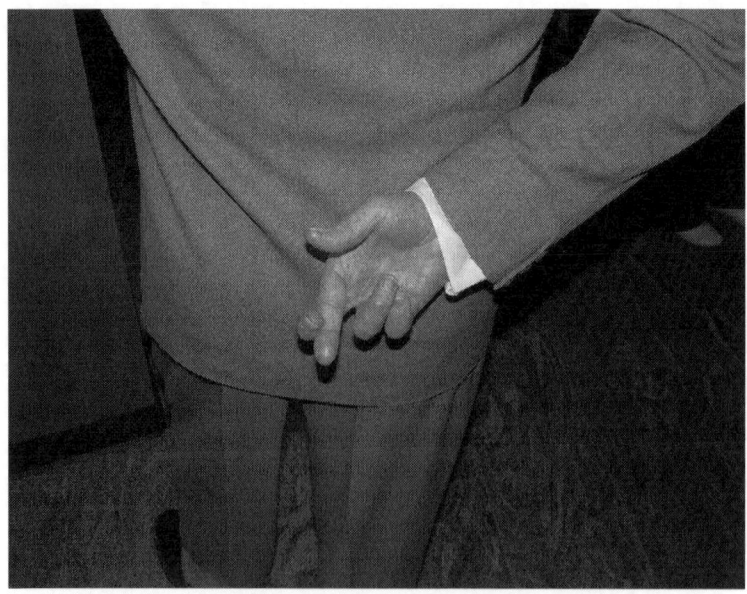

Lying is risky behavior and is not always guaranteed to produce the desired outcome in a situation. Photo courtesy of www.pixabay.com

I assume that I am much like most people in the sense that I severely dislike being subjected to lies and dishonesty. In addition to the prospect of being lied to, I also dislike the idea of having to lie when my personal reputation and integrity is put on the line. However, despite my upbringing, personal beliefs, and values, I would not hesitate to lie to protect my family.

Generally, the practice of lying is not looked upon favorably. However, there are definite times where such behavior is crucial and necessary for both practical and survival reasons.

Reasons for Subterfuge

Lying to protect self
Lying to protect others

Common Methods of Subterfuge and Deception

Misdirection
Dissimulation
False Testimony
False Statements
False Evidence
Truth Omission
Posturing
Feigning
Sleight of Hand
Camouflage

Because lying and subterfuge go against many of the formative teachings we receive regarding honesty and trustworthiness, it's a behavior in which most people do not excel. One almost has to delve into a life of criminal activity or enlist in government agencies to learn the skill-set in order to implement it into the tradecraft of espionage, intelligence, or counter-intelligence. Not only is it applied and implemented in espionage tradecraft, but it is also used as a method of detection in police investigations and interrogations.

Despite this, it is still a necessary component to behavioral camouflage and understanding both its relevance and role assists in the subsequent employment and detection of the tactic.

One of the most effective ways to learn the techniques is role-play in realistic situationally-based scenarios, get involved in a local theater troupe, or enroll in acting classes. All of these provide safe environments to practice, with the advantage that one is highly encouraged to portray roles with authenticity and intensity. Trying to practice these techniques in any other real-life environments subjects all parties involved in consequences that are detrimental to mutual trust, job security, and healthy relationships.

"The trust of the innocent is the liar's most useful tool."
- Stephen King

Citations:

[1] https://www.quora.com/What-is-Taqiyya-in-Islam-When-do-Muslims-practice-it
[2] https://www.al-islam.org/shiite-encyclopedia-ahlul-bayt-dilp-team/al-taqiyya-dissimulation-part-1
[3] Matthew 5:42, *King James Bible*

CHAPTER FIFTEEN

SUBCONSCIOUS

My first introduction to the body's subconscious response to interviewing techniques came in college as I was earning my Associates of Applied Sciences Degree in Criminal Justice. One of the required courses was Interviews and Interrogations. This is where I first heard of the various facial and eye movement "tells" indicating whether an individual is lying or telling the truth.

My fellow classmates and I would take turns playing the role of both interrogator and suspect, with each role receiving instruction from the professor regarding the deception to employ or which interrogation method/line of questioning to use.

Playing poker exposes several subconscious body language clues. Photo courtesy www.pixabay.com

Just as in poker and other card games, each player has behaviors that have the potential to alert the other players. Some people are quite accomplished at reading other people and can discover another's tell. All while masking and suppressing their own tells. To further complicate matters, the practice of bluffing or sending false tells is also going on at the same time. The James Bond movie, *Casino Royale*, gives an introductory snapshot of these practices, as well as any of the televised poker tournaments on cable television.

Later, I discovered the thriller novels of Brad Thor. The protagonist and hero throughout Thor's book series is Scot Harvath, a former Navy SEAL and ex-Secret Service agent who takes on clandestine missions to rid the world of global terrorists. The character had experience recognizing the "micro-expressions" of his various adversaries. This goes beyond basic body language deciphering and focuses in on the nuances of eye shifts, twitches, and pupil dilation. All of these micro expressions are difficult to detect without practice and some baseline knowledge of the person in question.

The eyes are truly the window to the soul and provide much information when observed throughout a conversation. This is why several players of the earlier mentioned poker games wear sunglasses. They use this tactic to block opponents from reading subconscious signals and eye movements the player cannot control or is entirely cognizant of such movement.

The subconscious mind is the most difficult to overrule and re-program because of its very meaning: the action or response is so natural the conscious mind pays little or no attention to it. The amount of willful effort and determination to make this possible is difficult to pull off convincingly, let alone to a point of considered mastery.

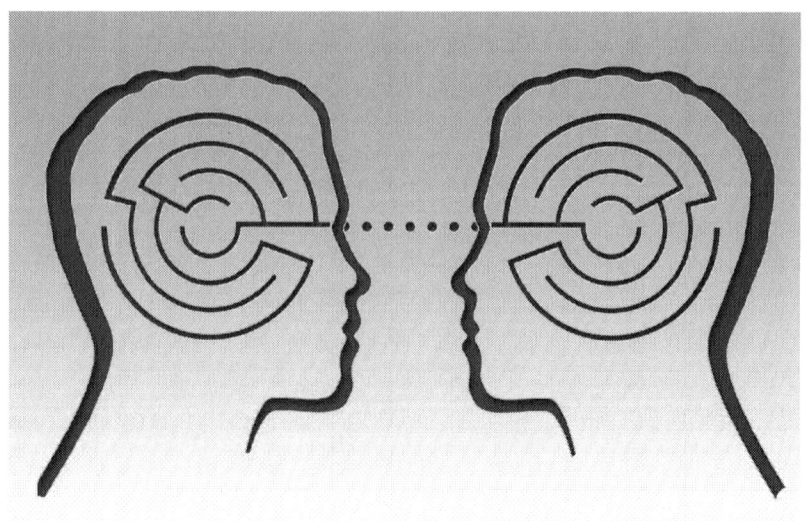

Every person we meet is gathering stimuli, regardless of their interpretation or their intent regarding the use of that collected stimuli. Photo courtesy of www.pixabay.com

Have you ever tried to inventory or consciously, purposely think about what you are doing and how you are doing it in regards to body language? This type of exercise will show you how and what kinds of stimuli you are potentially creating in the minds of others.

Let us look at the habit of biting one's fingernails and ask some specific questions regarding the behavior.

WHAT - What is fingernail biting? What does it look like? What does it sound like? What emotionally or environmentally triggers the behavior? What is its desired effect? What feelings are produced as a result from fingernail biting? What are the benefits? What are the consequences?

WHY - Why does the individual engage in fingernail biting? Why hasn't the individual chosen a different coping mechanism?

WHEN - When do the feelings or desire begin?

WHERE - Where is the habit done? Is it done publically, private? Is there a specific location or environment that serves as a triggering mechanism for the habit to manifest?

HOW - How does the habit alleviate the felt anxiety or reduce the stress? How is it initiated?

This example is not designed to over-complicate the habit, but rather deconstruct it into various components that one can apply to other signaling behaviors or habits. The purpose is to reduce or eliminate signaling cues from being picked up by others and exploited/used against you.

CONCLUSION

It is true that the very words we choose or do not use in our conversations have the potential to either obscure or advertise our intentions. The use of code words, foreign language, or combination of the two can also produce positive results or negative consequences.

The ongoing, intentional practice of OPSEC and PERSEC is one of diligence and vigilance. It requires the constant monitoring of those whom you share personal or mission-related information. Those deemed trustworthy once may not be that way a second time. Likewise, someone you do not know well now may earn your trust in the future.

Therefore, you must remain firm in your adherence to the principles, but aware of the tension and flex required to complete missions and maintain OPSEC and PERSEC.

A collage features the artwork of WWII era OPSEC posters. The warnings from past generations are still relevant today.

INTELLIGENCE GATHERING TERMS

HUMINT - Human Intelligence

SIGINT - Signals Intelligence

OSINT - Open Source Intelligence

GEOINT - Geospatial Intelligence

IMINT - Image Intelligence

MASINT - Measurement and Signature Intelligence

CYBINT - Cyber Intelligence

DNINT - Digital Network Intelligence

COMINT - Communications Intelligence

ELINT - Electronic Intelligence

TECHINT - Technical Intelligence

MEDINT - Medical Intelligence

FISINT - Foreign Instrumentation Signals Intelligence

FININT - Financial Intelligence

MARKINT - Market Intelligence

CULTINT - Culture Intelligence

ADDITIONAL RESOURCES

Alwood, Kelly, *Behavioral Programming: The Manipulation of Social Interaction*, 2015, CreateSpace Independent Publishing Platform

Bazzell, Michael, *Hiding from the Internet: Eliminating Personal Online Information*, 4th edition, CreateSpace Independent Publishing Platform, 2018

Bazzell, Michael, *The Complete Privacy and Security Desk Reference Vol. 1: Digital*, CreateSpace Independent Publishing Platform, 2016

Clark, Laura and Algaier, William, *Surveillance Detection: The Art of Prevention*, Cradle Press, LLC, 2007

Cooper, Jeff, *Principles of Personal Defense*, 1972 & 1989, Paladin Press

Hadnagy, Christopher, *Social Engineering: The Art of Human Hacking*, 2010, Wiley Publishing

Houston, Philip, Floyd, Michael, Carnicero, Susan, with Tennant, Don, *Spy the Lie: Former CIA Officers Teach You How to Detect Deception*, 2012, St. Martin's Press

Hughes, Chase, *The Ellipsis Manual: Analysis and Engineering of Human Behavior*, 2017, Evergreen Press

Inbau, Fred E., Reid, John E., Buckley, Joseph P., Jayne, Brian C., *Criminal Interrogation and Confessions*, 4th Ed., 2001, Aspen Publications

Lanier, Jaron, *Ten Arguments for Deleting Your Social Media Accounts Right Now*, Henry Holt & Company, 2018

Mack, Jefferson, *Invisible Resistance to Tyranny*, Paladin Press, 2002

McNnab, Chris, *The SAS Mental Endurance Handbook*, 2002, The Lyons Press

Mitnick, Kevin, with Varnosi, Robert, *The Art of Invisibility: The World's Most Famous Hacker Teaches You How to Be Safe in the Age of Big Brother and Big Data*, Little, Brown & Company, 2017

Narvarro, Joe, Poynter, Toni Sciarra, *Dangerous Personalities: An FBI Profiler Shows You How to Identify and Protect Yourself from Harmful People*, 2018, Rodale Books, reprint edition

Pease, Allan & Barbara, *The Definitive Book of Body Language*, 2006, Bantam Books

Schafer, Jack, Karlins, Marvin, *The Like Switch: An Ex-FBI Agent's Guide to Influencing, Attracting, and Winning People Over*, 2015, Touchstone

Sun Tzu, *The Art of War*, translated by Thomas Cleary, 1998, Shambhala Publications

ABOUT THE AUTHOR

This page intentionally left blank.

The previous page is a snarky example to prove my point of the book. It is not necessary to disclose information you are not comfortable or authorized to share, even if those around you insist or request the information.

Nevertheless, because it is customary for authors to provide a brief biography for those who really want to know...

Matthew Dermody is the author of three other books on various camouflage and concealment topics. He currently resides in overseas with his wife and children. He also has a vast collection of likes, dislikes, and strong opinions on a plethora of subjects that he often receives neither solicitations to discuss nor financial compensation when discussing.

Made in the USA
Middletown, DE
04 December 2018